H-O-T R-O-D

photographs by David Perry **story** by Barry Gifford

CHRONICLE BOOKS
SAN FRANCISCO

PHOTOGRAPHS COPYRIGHT © **1997** by David Perry
TEXT COPYRIGHT © **1997** by Barry Gifford
DESIGN by Martin Venezky

ALL RIGHTS RESERVED. **NO PART** OF THIS BOOK MAY BE REPRODUCED IN ANY FORM WITHOUT WRITTEN PERMISSION FROM THE PUBLISHER.
PRINTED IN HONG KONG.

LIBRARY OF CONGRESS CATALOGING-IN-PUBLICATION DATA:
Perry, David, 1959–
      Hot rod / photographs by David Perry; story by Barry Gifford.
        p.   cm.
      ISBN 0–8118–1593–5
      1. Hot rods—Pictorial works.   I. Gifford, Barry, 1946–
II. Title.
TL236.3.P465   1997
629.228—dc20   96–26779
                                  CIP

DISTRIBUTED IN CANADA BY
Raincoast Books
8680 Cambie Street
Vancouver, B.C. V6P 6M9

10 9 8 7 6 5 4 3 2 1

Chronicle Books
85 Second Street
San Francisco, CA 94105

WEB SITE: www.chronbooks.com

for **mary**

PAY LESS THAN EVER for a Star

Romántica Barry Gifford

YOLANDA HAD A THUMBNAIL-SIZE SCAR HIGH ON HER LEFT CHEEK.
When Danny inquired about it she turned sullen and the pink mark became crimson. A shudder, visible to Danny, passed through the length of her body, concluding with a brief facial twist and audible soft gasp. At the moment, the two were semi-entwined, standing under a xanthic desert moon in front of Yolanda's Airstream in East Bakersfield.

"You know what day this is?" asked Yolanda.

"February 29th," he said. "Had a extra day before rent's due."

"El día de Santa Niña de las Putas, the patron saint of Satan's prisoners. It comes only when there's a second full moon in the month on the final day of February in a leap year."

"Knew about the blue moon. Never heard of Satan's prisoners, though."

"Those are souls sold to Satan during the person's lifetime. People who reformed before their death and tried to undo the deal."

Danny disentwined himself, lit a Lucky, inhaled, coughed. The night air felt chilly now that he wasn't pressed against Yolanda. He rubbed his hands together then shoved them into his pants pockets, letting the cigarette dangle from between his lips.

"Who was Santa Niña?" he mumbled.

"A romántica, like me, born in Jalisco. Her father had bargained with the devil in order to save the life of his wife, who was dying from a cancer. Satan told him his wife would live only if the man promised also the souls of his three sons."

"Not the daughter?"

"Niña was not yet born. She was the youngest of four children. The father was horrified to do this but consented, thinking that later he could persuade Satan not to take his sons. The mother recovered and, of course, no matter how passionately her husband begged, the devil would not relent. The thought that he and his sons were doomed to hell destroyed the poor man, and he died of grief soon after the birth of his daughter."

"Did the mother know about this deal?"

"Not until her husband confessed on his deathbed. When Niña was twelve years old her brothers were killed when a donkey cart in which they were riding broke its axle on a steep mountain road and crashed with the donkey to the bottom of a ravine. Niña's mother then told her about the fate of the boys' souls, so the girl vowed to save them and her father."

Danny spat out the cigarette. "Did she?"

"Yes. That night she called to Satan, telling him she could not live without her brothers, that she wanted to join them immediately. When Satan appeared she took his hand and allowed him to lead her to hell, where she became his mistress."

Suddenly Danny no longer felt the cold. Yolanda had put on a tape of old rock and roll songs in the trailer. Chuck Willis's "Betty and Dupree" was playing. Chuck sang, "Dupree told Betty, I'll buy you anything."

"Satan's attachment to Niña was soon complete," said Yolanda. "She beguiled him in ways even the King of Cruelty had never imagined. In this way was it possible for her to gain a kind of power over the devil and convince him to allow her father and brothers to pass out of hell and enter into the King-dom of Heaven. Niña, of course, had to remain in hell as Satan's whore. It is the prostitutes who honor her on this, the rarest of days, for her sacrifice."

"Saint Niña of the Whores."

"Our own and only. This is the one day no whore should feel ashamed in the eyes of God."

"But what about your scar? How did you get it?"

"After I made it with a man for money for the first time I cut myself on the face with a sharp edge of a rock."

"But why? You were so beautiful. You still are."

"To never be so beautiful again. I was marked inside and out."

Danny embraced her. "My poor Yolanda."

She pulled away and glared at him. "No," she said, "there is nothing about me that is poor."

DANNY SAT IN HIS SHORT LOOKING OUT AT THE SAND HILLS TO THE SOUTHEAST. The day was fading fast. He lit a Lucky and listened to the long, lugubrious, wobbly whistle of the southbound Hi-Ball. Danny had grown used to this scorching cry from the evening freight. "La Expresa tristeza" the locals called it, or "El Tormento." Every day at 6:56 P.M., they said, *la horca del diablo* — the devil's pitchfork — was driven a bit deeper into the soul. Danny had begun to believe it, expecting but never quite being prepared for the whistle. He was always taken by surprise.

Waiting for Yolanda was not easy for him. As a child Danny had often accompanied his daddy, Big Danny, on his rounds of the Bakersfield area bars. While Big Danny drank and caroused, Danny was made to sit outside on the curb or in the pickup, sometimes for hours at a time, staring at and being stared at by passersby. Sometimes kids picked fights with him, older kids, and Danny often had to run away and sneak back later, hoping that his father had not left him behind. Big Danny's *juerga* inevitably ended in a brawl. Danny's abiding mental picture of his daddy — who died of a stab wound to the chest when Danny was sixteen — was Big Danny's bloodied face as he stumbled out of some dive. Danny always told people who asked that his daddy had died from a heart attack. He never told them that Big Danny's heart had been attacked with a blade wielded by a drunken coyote in a shitkicker bar called Rowdy Dave's Dream of Paradise.

Danny's mother, Lee Ella, had died from pneumonia when the boy was four. He barely remem-bered her. Big Danny, who stood four foot eleven and one-quarter inch without his boots, was a legendary figure on the midget rodeo circuit from Chula Vista to San Jose. His best event, before alcoholism forced him to quit, had been bull riding. Big Danny made his bones beating the clock at

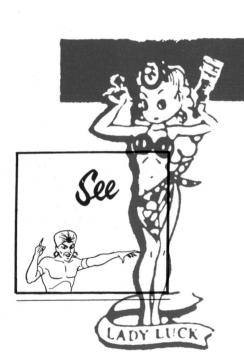

H-O-T R-O-D

photographs by David Perry **story** by Barry Gifford

CHRONICLE BOOKS

SAN FRANCISCO

DESIGN by Martin Venezky

PRINTED IN HONG KONG.

LIBRARY OF CONGRESS CATALOGING-IN-PUBLICATION DATA:
Perry, David, 1959–
Hot rod / photographs by David Perry; story by Barry Gifford.
p. cm.
ISBN 0–8118–1593–5
1. Hot rods—Pictorial works. I. Gifford, Barry, 1946–
II. Title.
TL236.3.P465 1997
629.228—dc20 96–26779
CIP

DISTRIBUTED IN CANADA BY
Raincoast Books
8680 Cambie Street
Vancouver, B.C. V6P 6M9

10 9 8 7 6 5 4 3 2 1

Chronicle Books
85 Second Street
San Francisco, CA 94105

WEB SITE: www.chronbooks.com

Stockton on a terrible beast named Nasty At Night. When he wasn't rodeoing, Big Danny worked construction and did odd jobs. Danny had been on his own since his daddy's death. Until his infatuation with Yolanda Ríos, he'd kept clear of attachments. Now he was waiting again.

*　*　*　*　*　*

DANNY DECIDED TO FORTIFY HIMSELF BEFORE HAVING IT OUT WITH YOLANDA. He drove out past Famoso and stopped at a bar named El Lagarto Tuerto. Danny's left bootheel hit the sand just as a corona discharge gyrated onto a telephone pole next to the highway. Danny ducked back into his Cutlass as he watched St. Elmo's fire roll along the line like an acrobat riding a bicycle on a high wire. The blue-white lightning ball danced daintily on its silent path for several seconds, then disappeared as rapidly as it had come, leaving only a path of mist in its wake. There had been no thunder or noise other than a faint hiss following the sphere's decay.

Danny waited a few moments before again attempting to disembark. He recalled having read in *UFO Monthly,* a magazine he'd found lying around Chifla Miguel's Chop Shop, that ball lightning was often misidentified as a spaceship. In fact, it was gas or air behaving in an unusual way, powered perhaps by a high-frequency electro-magnetic field or focused cosmic ray particles. As he lowered his leg again to the ground, Danny heard thunder, and he hurried toward the bar before the rain came. Thunderstorms, he knew, functioned as batteries to keep the earth charged negatively and the atmosphere charged positively.

Danny reached the entrance just as several tons of water hit the earth in his immediate vicinity. As far as it being a good or bad omen, he couldn't tell. Danny only hoped that God knew what He was doing, because he wasn't too sure about himself.

There were only two customers inside, both seated on barstools since there were no tables and chairs. Danny stood at the bar for two minutes but no bartender appeared. He turned to the patron nearest him and was about to ask if someone were working, but the man was sound asleep, snoring with his head resting on his arms on the counter. Danny shifted his attention to a black-bearded man at the opposite end who sat staring at the label of a beer bottle in front of him.

"Hey, pardner," Danny said, "anybody servin'?"

The man did not respond.

"Hey, buddy. Amigo! I asked, anybody work here?"

The customer so addressed promptly fell off of his barstool, out of Danny's sight.

"Jesus, what a place," he said.

He could hear the storm raging outside, loud thunder and heavy rain. Nevertheless, Danny turned toward the door.

"Welcome to the One-Eyed Lizard!" boomed a voice behind him.

Danny did a one-eighty and saw a white-haired woman who stood well over six feet tall. She had a hawk nose and eyes that went with it. The woman was wearing a checkered shirt and bluejeans held up by red suspenders spread wide by her enormous bosom. Danny pegged her age at fifty-five, give or take a few.

"You want a drink or not?" she barked.

Danny returned to the bar. "I didn't see anybody workin'."

"You see someone now. What'll it be?"

"Negra Modelo, I guess."

The large woman squinted, taking a closer look at him.

"You're a cloudy boy, all right."

"Cloudy?"

"Not too certain about yourself."

She produced a bottle of beer, cracked it open, and placed it on the bar in front of Danny, where it foamed over on the counter.

"How can you tell?" he asked.

The woman snorted. "There's even more I can't — won't — tell ya. I've got the gift."

"The gift?"

"The gift of seein' both the present and the future at the same time. See my eyes?"

Danny stared at them. Both were pale blue with extraordinarily dilated pupils.

"A seer, son. Same as Amos, Asaph, Gad, Heman, Samual, and Zadok. You heard of them, ain't ya?"

"No, ma'am."

"What do you do, boy?"

"Work on cars. Race 'em, too."

She stared directly at Danny, leaning forward, her large hands pressing down hard on the bar. Her right eye wandered, jerked, rolled around. Danny watched it move.

"Your right eye the one sees the future?"

The woman leaned back. Her eye calmed down.

"Break thou the arm of the wicked and the evil man," she said. "Seek out his wickedness till thou find none."

"Yes, ma'am."

"Drink up and go."

Danny took a long swig from the bottle, set it back down on the counter, and pulled a dollar from his pocket.

"No charge," the woman said. "Go your way. I send you forth as a lamb among wolves."

Danny ran through the rain to his car, got in, and sat there thinking about what the woman had said. Suddenly, a single vertical bolt of cloud-to-ground lightning exited as a bright pink spot atop the thunderhead. It struck the tin roof of El Lagarto Tuerto, igniting the Cutlass's engine. Danny sat in the idling automobile, trembling. It was time to find Yolanda.

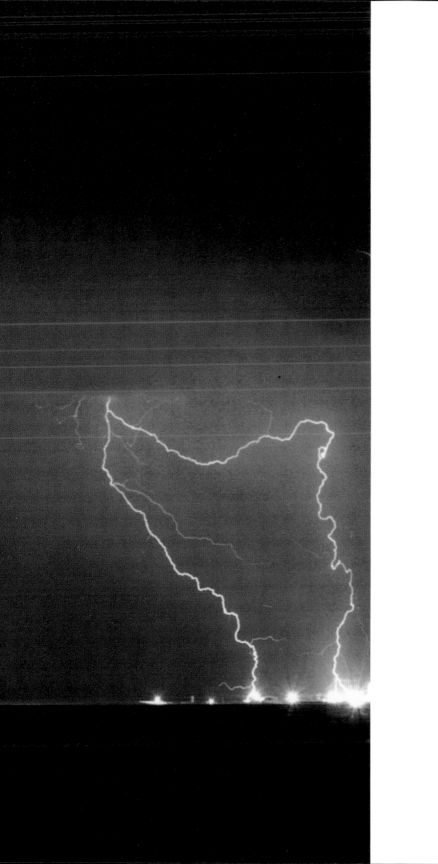

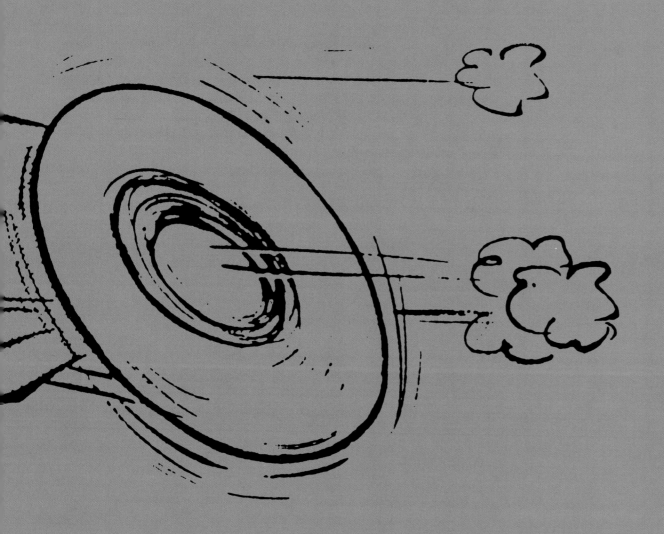

chop **shop**

NO. **1**

NO. **3**

NO. **9**

OVERHAUL YOU[R]
MOTOR IN **10**

CLEANSE
with "MOTO

Von Francis ©

CHROME

NO. **27**

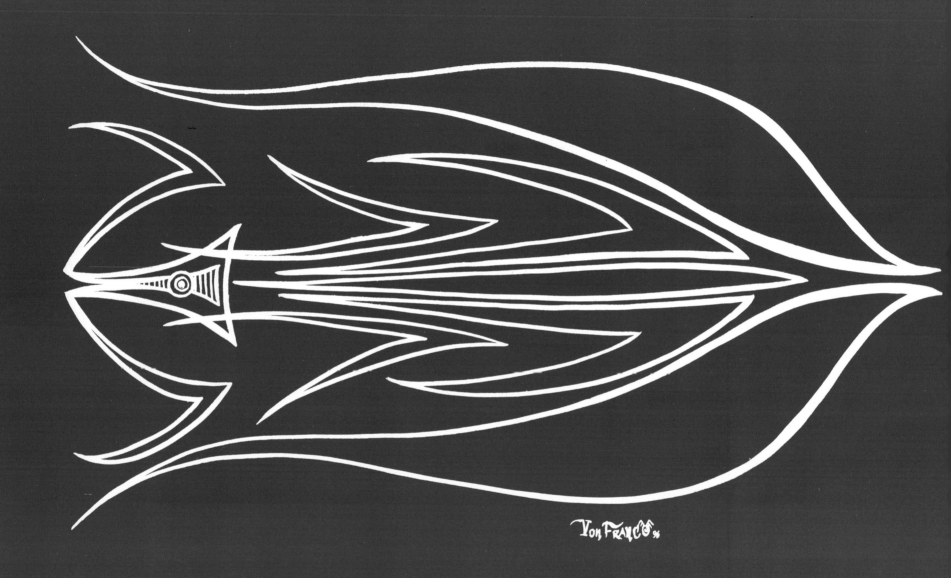

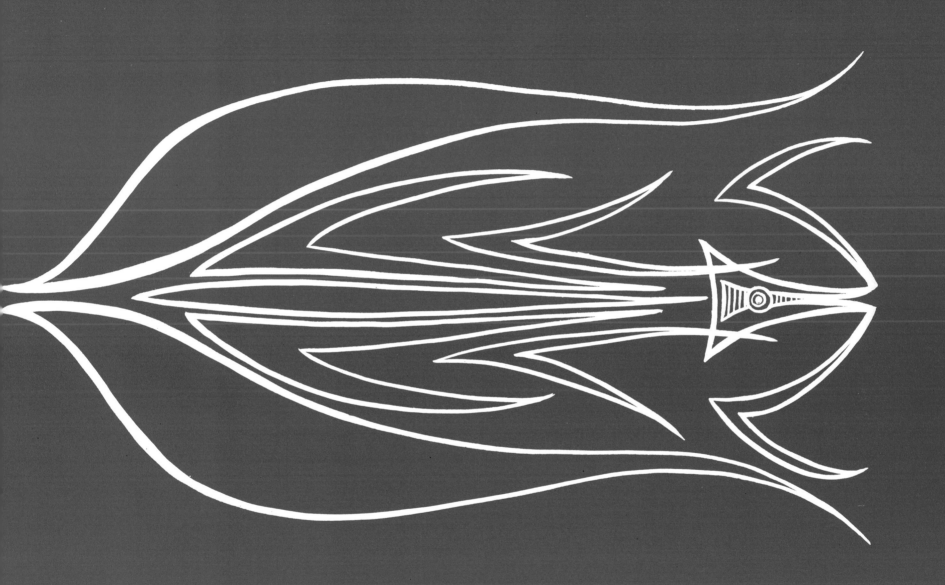

bonneville and **el mirage**

NO. **36**

SPEED G

Division of Arrow Aut

00 Washington Ave. No., Min

JACKET EMBLE

15

Multi-colored
lems and decal
nearly every s
wool felt scree
assorted colors—

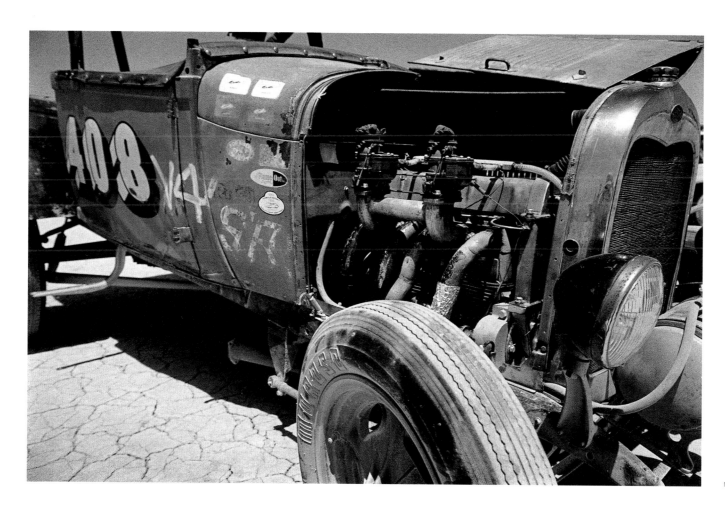

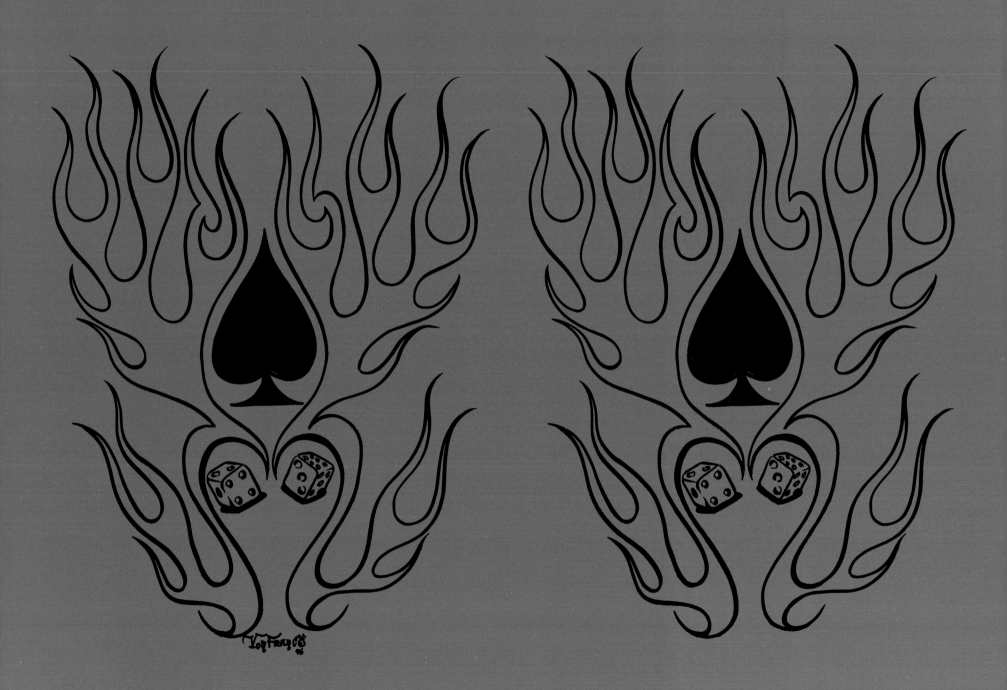

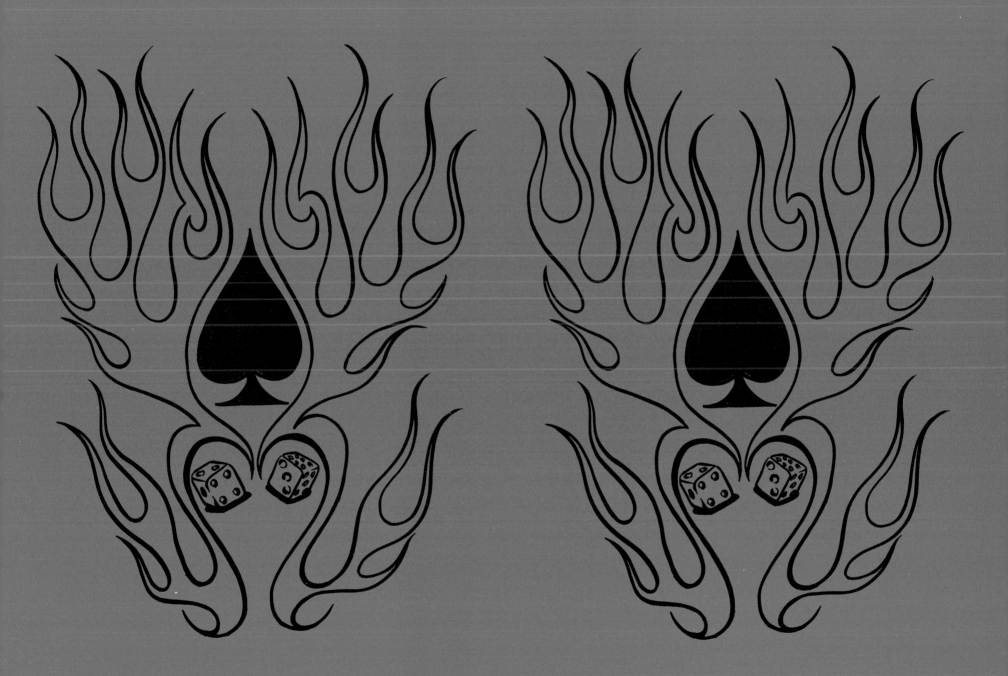

NO. **50**

* * * * * *

FREE
"HOW TO"
CATALOG

POWER!   ECONOMY!
STYLE!

— — — — MAIL ORDER NOW — — — —

WE DECIDED THAT THE WORLD'S MAGNIFICENCE HAS BEEN
enriched by a new beauty, the beauty of speed—

A racing car, who's hood is adorned with great pipes
like serpents of explosive breath...

We want to hymn the man at the wheel who hurls the lance
of his spirit across the earth,
along the circle of its orbit.

F.T. MARINETTI FROM
THE FUTURIST MANIFESTO
OF **1909**

NO. **58**

NO. **63**

SPEED

NO. **65**

NO. **66**

NO. **67**

POWER-SPEED!

- Action
- Performance
- Wear

NO. **68**

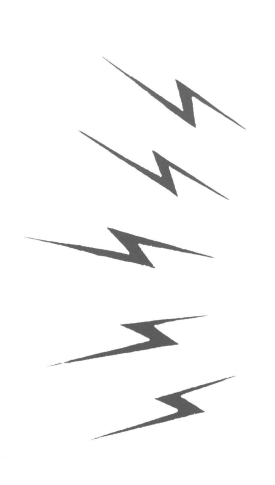

NO. **74**

list of plates

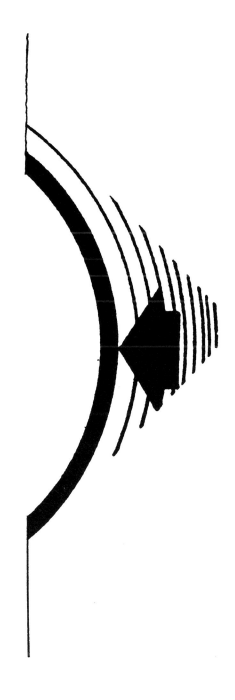

You'll
HAVE A REAL HOT

ROD LIBRARY

GET MORE POWER

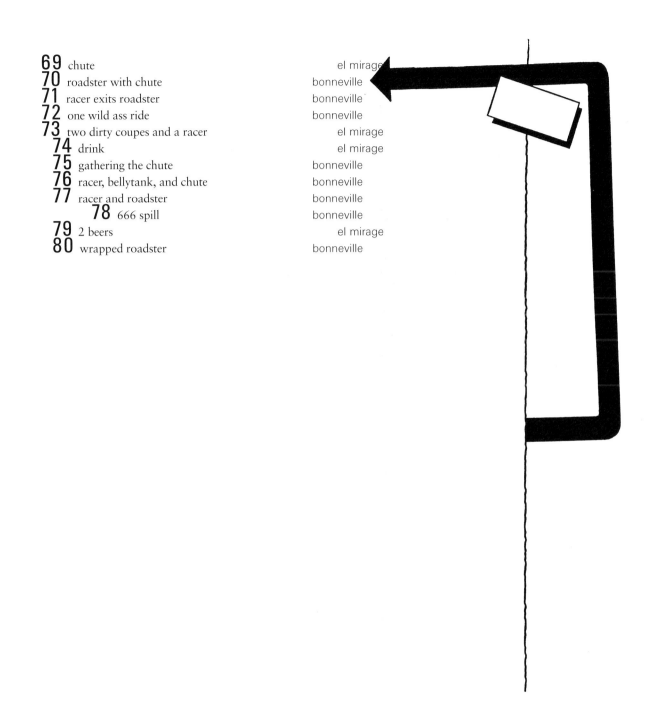

* * * * * * *

ACKNOWLEDGEMENTS A truckload of thanks to all the
speed-crazed kids living in a souped-up jungle of crazy thrills
I have had the pleasure to know these
past few years . . .

quintessential hot rodders squeek bell, paul borrmann and kindred spirit "sneaky" pete nash, for showing me the sacred garage and demonstrating what really makes a gow job; dragstrip-beatniks keith weesner, "johnny ford" stodd, chris harvey, abe freeman, kirk jones, verne hammond, tony castaneda, kevan sledge, darby "preacher boy" patterson and rockabilly queens robin "jezebel" white, kassy mays, mercedes cory, jessica brooks, jalopy jockey diana coopersmith, and salt racer jodi lawshe, for trusting me with their likeness and giving the project a face; board of advisors ed "big daddy" roth, robert williams, jerry desvaux at *continental restyling*, and rob fortier and jerry weesner at *street rodder* for giving me the thumbs up on the project; rescue photographers and drinking buddies walter cotten and steven de pinto—for their rowdy bonneville campsites, rambling hot rod dialog and generous supply of amber fluids; kevin thatcher and the gang at *juxtapoz* for including me in their fine publication; roger farley hillyard for hosting my first hot rod exhibit; brad bunnin for his expert legal assistance; fred dodsworth of *au juice* magazine for connecting me with barry; barry gifford for his rockin' poetic fiction reaction piece; martin venezky for the full k-u-s-t-o-m design; maya hayuk, smokie, bruce gossett, and "jumpin" jake atlee for the bitchin' flame job, von franco for the pinstriping, chester "grampa" klock for the swell cartoons; hipsters craig olsen, eric "vic vegas" kiertzner, melissa "giggles" fry, and ernie "chopper" hernandez for their numerous acts of generosity; my uncle "lucky" for turning me on to cool cars, smokin' soul bro' mark johann for the roadtrips and the cubans; rita damore for her cosmic love and design excellence; caroline herter, emily miller, michael carabetta, and sarah bolles at chronicle books for believing in lowbrow art d'elegance and making my dream a reality; mike carson and southern california timing association, mary wells and the utah salt flats racing association, and all the racers, families and crews—they're what this book is all about; and lastly, my bride, mary, who has listened to gearhead jargon, put up with greasy car parts on the kitchen table and believed in my hot-rods-from-hell idea. my love to y'all. save the salt.

— DAVID PERRY